AF200185

GOLF MENTAL COINS

ISBN: 978-3-7481-6730-3

Production and publishing: Book on Demand GmbH, Norderstedt / Germany

1st edition (2018)

Copyright: Heiko Hansen

The Basic:
„Golf Dynamic Breathing"

The University of Chicago was able to demonstrate in a study that golfers who think as little as possible about the game and need less time for the shot are more successful. They almost play hypno-golf. In training it is recommended to use the breathing technique twice per putt in order to achieve a corresponding number of repetitions. Always: At the beginning in the strategy box (behind the ball) and at the beginning in the play box.

In competition you only need to use the breathing technique once. Either at the end of the strategy box before you go into the play box. Or, at the beginning of the play box, if necessary with a view to the hole or target location of the ball.

GOLF DYNAMIC BREATHING
Inhale 4 seconds incl. diaphragm, stop briefly, then exhale with a short roll of the shoulders backwards and ring in the chest a little.
Exhale for 4 seconds and the shoulders accompany the breathing downwards.

It is extremely important to feel an inner sense of well-being and emotional-mental confidence when exhaling. The thought and the cognitive mental preparation is only as much value as you can create and feel this feeling. In addition, the quality of the exercise is only worth as much and the effect in the tournament can be produced the more intensively you have trained beforehand.

If you feel tired during the competition, then sprinkle several 2-3 seconds of breathing in between the strokes and push yourself. It is also helpful to knead both auricles from top to bottom several times vigorously up and down. This activates many energizing meridians.

Advantage:
- *More inner peace (emotion control)*
- *more self-confidence and self-efficacy (self-confidence)*
- *increased mental condition and focus (attention regulation)*
- *improved access to the unconscious (e.g. place of all your experiences and talents).*

Mental Putts (MP)

Specifications

- Always perform breathing „Golf Dynamic Breathing" correctly
  a. In the strategy box (behind the ball) and
  b. in the play box (on the ball) breathe once, best three times.

- When exhaling, use your mental film to play the ball into the hole. You can look at the hole or where it is most comfortable for you. When exhaling, successfully putt the ball in front of your mental eye until the ball falls into the hole. Hear the plop-pen with your inner ear.

- Recommendation: min. 10 passes

- **Mental Coins:** 1 point per success.
  If all balls were pocketed by the player in a MC exercise, then there are 10 extra coins, e.g. 10 of 10 putts.

  More extra points for 50 possible putts:
  All Putts in = 10 Coins (100%)
  47 - 49 = 7 Coins (mind. 94% - 99,9%)
  45 - 46 = 5 Coins (90 - 93,9%)

- Any MP exercise can also be done with the non-dominant hand or play with one hand or as PRO.

- Your golf trainer can change the target (total number of successful putts) for the training.

- **Speed-Variant:**
  - SV 1: The player has 5 seconds standing on the ball to putt.
  - SV 2: The player has 3 seconds standing on the ball to putt.
  - SV 3: The player must complete the exercise within 15 minutes as many complete successful putts as possible. Incl. breathing.
  - SV 4: The player must complete the exercise within a certain period

of time, e.g. xx putts in 15 minutes.

Forecast-Variant / Prognosis

- Golf trainers gives a forecast which the player must achieve,
  e.g. at least 45 of 50 Putts, otherwise 10 Coins will be lost from the
  the number of points reached was subtracted.

MP 1:

- From one club length, from five positions play around the hole, mark with a tee and lay out 5 balls
- Variables: play from 2 - 4 club lengths

MP 2:

- Mark one playing position and lay out three balls one after the other in three racket lengths.

MP 3:

- Mark a playing position with four racket lengths in a row and lay out four balls.

MP 4:

- Mark a playing position with five club lengths one behind the other and lay out five balls.

MP 5:

- You place five tees around the hole in five different directions, in one to five club lengths.

MP 6:

- Throw five balls in different directions around the hole. They start by putting the ball that is next to the hole. This must be at least one club length away from the hole.

MP 7:

- Throw eight balls around the hole and play the putts alternately with a teammate.

MP 8:

- Like MP3 or MP7 + dealing with interference.
- Coach or player creates a disturbance when the player is in the play-box. The moment of disturbance can be the training partner choose. Also the way: Question, pin in the putt track throw, lift ball, clear throat. It may only be disturbed once per putt.
- The other player must then immediately take a step out of his preparation and concentrate anew. Then take a deep breath and restart the MP exercise.

MP 9:

- Two balls are placed around four holes and marked with tees. The direction can be chosen freely.
  The first tee is set in two club lengths.
  The second in three club lengths.
- The player plays both balls and then goes to the next hole.

MP 10:

- Like MP9. Four players alternating clockwise from hole to hole, playing both balls and then the balls to the tees. And put it back.

Training Results: **Mental Putts**

DATE	EXERCISE, opt. plus speed / forecast	ROUNDS	RESULTS COINS	Mentalcoins, Opt. Extracoins	TOTAL

Training Results: **Mental Putts**

DATE	EXERCISE, opt. plus speed / forecast	ROUNDS	RESULTS COINS	Mentalcoins, Opt. Extracoins	TOTAL

Training Results: **Mental Putts**

DATE	EXERCISE, opt. plus speed / forecast	ROUNDS	RESULTS COINS	Mentalcoins, Opt. Extracoins	TOTAL

Training Results: **Mental Putts**

DATE	EXERCISE, opt. plus speed / forecast	ROUNDS	RESULTS COINS	Mentalcoins, Opt. Extracoins	TOTAL

Training Results: **Mental Putts**

DATE	EXERCISE, opt. plus speed / forecast	ROUNDS	RESULTS COINS	Mentalcoins, Opt. Extracoins	TOTAL

Training Results: **Mental Putts**

DATE	EXERCISE, opt. plus speed / forecast	ROUNDS	RESULTS COINS	Mentalcoins, Opt. Extracoins	TOTAL

Pirat Putts (PP)

Specifications

- Basis "Mental Putts" exercises incl. additional points.
  Description: PP1 - PP10

- The dominant eye is covered with an eye patch during putt.
  You play with the non-dominant eye.

- My dominant eye is: O right O left.

- 40 putts with the non-dominant eye.

- Variation 1:
  20 putts with the non-dominant eye,
  then 20 putts with the dominant eye.

- Variation 2:
  Prognosis specification by your golf trainer

- Variation 3:
  Speed version

Training Results: **Pirat Putts**

DATE	EXERCISE, opt. plus speed / forecast	ROUNDS	RESULTS COINS	Mentalcoins, Opt. Extracoins	TOTAL

Training Results: **Pirat Putts**

DATE	EXERCISE, opt. plus speed / forecast	ROUNDS	RESULTS COINS	Mentalcoins, Opt. Extracoins	TOTAL

Training Results: **Pirat Putts**

DATE	EXERCISE, opt. plus speed / forecast	ROUNDS	RESULTS COINS	Mentalcoins, Opt. Extracoins	TOTAL

www.golfmentalhandicap.com

Training Results: **Pirat Putts**

DATE	EXERCISE, opt. plus speed / forecast	ROUNDS	RESULTS COINS	Mentalcoins, Opt. Extracoins	TOTAL

Training Results: **Pirat Putts**

DATE	EXERCISE, opt. plus speed / forecast	ROUNDS	RESULTS COINS	Mentalcoins, Opt. Extracoins	TOTAL

Training Results: **Pirat Putts**

DATE	EXERCISE, opt. plus speed / forecast	ROUNDS	RESULTS COINS	Mentalcoins, Opt. Extracoins	TOTAL

Winning Putts (WP)

Specifications

- Two players always play against each other and face each other.

- Integrate the "Golf Dynamic Breathing" into your routine.
  "Golf Dynamic Breathing" is only used once on the ball.
  In case of disregard 1 coin will be deducted.

- Each successful putt = 1 coin.

- The winner gets 10 extra coins.

- In some WP variants, minus points are also possible.

- The ball is returned to the tee by the player after the putt.

- Variation 1:
  Instead of 6 tees, your golf trainer can also determine 8 or 10 tees.

- Variation 2:
  Your golf trainer can set different distances between the balls:
  0,5m / 1,0m / 1,5m / 2,0m / 2,5m

- Variation 3:
  Specification by your golf trainer, how many putts have to fall, other-wise the extra coins for the winner are omitted if the minimum putts have not been reached.

WP 1:

- 6 tees in a circle 2.0m away from the hole in the green.
- Stand on one tee and your opponent stands on one tee opposite you, so that two tees are free between each of them.
- The task now is to catch up with your opponent. Then the game is over and the overtaken player has lost.
- For each punched putt you move one tee forward counterclockwise. If you push a putt past, this is not bad at first. You simply stop at the tea.
- If you have punched so many putts that you are one tee further than your partner - i.e. you have overtaken him - you have won.

WP 2:

- Like MP1 + a match is finished after 10 minutes.
- If no winner is determined, the player who is closer to the partner wins again and gets the *extra coins*.

WP 3:

- Like WP 2.
- This time you fall back one tee for every putt you push past, up to your maximum starting point. If you are then caught, then you have lost.
- The maximum time allowed for a match is 10 minutes.
- If no one has caught up with the other, the player closer to the partner wins again, i.e. the player who has punched more putts wins.

WP 4:

- 8 tees around the hole in two alternately different distances: 4 tees 1,0m, 4 tees 1,5m.
- 15 minutes time
- Whoever makes the most putts wins.

WP 5:

- 8 tees around the hole in two alternately different distances: 4 tees 1,5m, 4 tees 2,0m.
- 15 minutes time
- Whoever makes the most putts wins.

WP 6:

- 8 tees around the hole in four alternately different distances: 2 tees 0,5m, 1,0m, 1,5m, 2.0m each.
- 15 minutes time
- Whoever makes the most putts wins.

WP 7:

- 8 tees around the hole in two alternately different distances: 4 tees 1,0m, 4 tees 1,5m.
- Each missed putt = 1 MinusCoin.
- 15 minutes time.
- Whoever achieves the most putts wins.

WP 8:

- 8 tees around the hole in two alternately different distances: 4 tees 1,0m, 4 tees 1,5m.
- Each missed putt = 1 MinusCoin.
- 15 minutes time.
- Whoever achieves the most putts wins.
- If you finish with minus points, you also collect 5 minus points.

WP 9:

- 8 tees around the hole in two alternately different distances: 4 tees 1,0m, 4 tees 1,5m.
- The *dominant eye* is covered with an eye patch.
- 10 minutes time.
- Whoever achieves the most putts wins.

WP 10:

- 8 tees around the hole in two alternately different distances: 4 tees 1,0m, 4 tees 1,5m.
- Each player may disturb his fellow player 3 times.
- 10 minutes time.
- Whoever achieves the most putts wins.

Training Results: **Winning Putts**

DATE	EXERCISE	RESULTs/ COINS	DATE	EXERCISE	RESULTs/ COINS

Training Results: **Winning Putts**

DATE	EXERCISE	RESULTs/ COINS	DATE	EXERCISE	RESULTs/ COINS

Training Results: **Winning Putts**

DATE	EXERCISE	RESULTs/ COINS	DATE	EXERCISE	RESULTs/ COINS

Training Results: **Winning Putts**

DATE	EXERCISE	RESULTs/ COINS	DATE	EXERCISE	RESULTs/ COINS

Training Results: **Winning Putts**

DATE	EXERCISE	RESULTs/ COINS	DATE	EXERCISE	RESULTs/ COINS

Training Results: **Winning Putts**

DATE	EXERCISE	RESULTs/ COINS	DATE	EXERCISE	RESULTs/ COINS

Blind Putts

Specifications

- You putt with your eyes closed.
  Buy a sleep mask or two pirates/eye patches!

- The aim of this exercise is for you to trust and feel 100% in your preparation for the putt and the movement itself. This will result in a faster
  automatism. Unsafe putters sometimes look at the hole before putting
  and hope that the ball will successfully find its way to the hole.

- Integrate „Golf Dynamic Breathing" into your routine.

- „Golf Dynamic Breathing" is only applied once on the ball.

- In case of disregard 1 coin will be deducted.

- Recommended: 10 passes.

- Every successful putt BP 1-6 brings one coin.

- Each successful putt BP 7 brings 10 coins.

- Each successful putt BP 8 brings 20 coins.

- Variation 1:
  Memorize the putting line on the ball, then remove the sleeping mask
  and putt blindly.

- Variation 2:
  Emboss the putt on the ball with one view of the hole and ball. Then
  align the head on the ball and do not move the head during the putt.
  Only after three seconds the head may be moved.

BP 1:

- Place 4 tees in racket lengths or 1.0m behind each other.
- You can determine the direction of the hole yourself.
- Emboss the putt on the ball with a view of the hole. Then align the head on the ball and do not move the head during the putt. Only after three seconds the head may be moved.

BP 2:

- 8 tees around the hole in two alternately different distances: 4 tees 1,0m, 4 tees 1,5m.
- Emboss the putt on the ball with a view of the hole. Then align the head on the ball and do not move the head during the putt. Only after three seconds the head may be moved.

BP 3:

- 8 tees around the hole in four alternating different distances: 2 tees each 0.5m, 1.0m, 1.5m, 2.0m.
- Emboss the putt on the ball with a view of the hole. Then align the head on the ball and do not move the head during the putt. Only after three seconds the head may be moved.

BP 4:

- Place 4 tees in bat lengths or 1.0m behind each other.
- You can determine the orientation of the clubs yourself.
- Memorize the putting line on the ball, then pull down the sleeping mask and putt blindly.

BP 5:

- 8 tees around the hole in two alternately different distances: 4 tees 1,0m, 4 tees 1,5m.
- Memorize the putting line on the ball, then pull down the sleeping mask and putt blindly.

BP 6:

- 8 tees around the hole in four alternating different distances:
- 2 tees 0,5m, 1,0m, 1,5m, 2.0m each.
- Memorize the putting line on the ball, then pull down the sleeping mask and putt blindly.

BP 7:

- Two players, 10 putts each. Change every 2 putts.
- The seeing player places the ball in a range of 1.0m around the hole.
- The blind player (the entire time with a sleep mask or 2 eye patches) must find the ball, feel the putting line, go to the ball and play.
- Each successful putt brings 10 coins.

BP 8:

- Two players, 10 putts each. Change every 2 putts.
- The seeing player places the ball in a range of 1.5m around the hole.
- The blind player (the entire time with a sleep mask or 2 eye patches) must find the ball, feel the putting line, go to the ball and play.
- Each successful putt brings 20 coins.

Training Results: **Blind Putts**

DATE	EXERCISE	RESULTs/ COINS	DATE	EXERCISE	RESULTs/ COINS

Training Results: **Blind Putts**

DATE	EXERCISE	RESULTs/ COINS	DATE	EXERCISE	RESULTs/ COINS

Training Results: **Blind Putts**

DATE	EXERCISE	RESULTs/ COINS	DATE	EXERCISE	RESULTs/ COINS

Training Results: **Blind Putts**

DATE	EXERCISE	RESULTs/ COINS	DATE	EXERCISE	RESULTs/ COINS

Training Results: **Blind Putts**

DATE	EXERCISE	RESULTs/ COINS	DATE	EXERCISE	RESULTs/ COINS

Training Results: **Blind Putts**

DATE	EXERCISE	RESULTs/ COINS	DATE	EXERCISE	RESULTs/ COINS

Chip & Putt (CP)

Specifications

- The chip on the green is then completed with one putt or two putts.

- Each successful putt counts 1 coin.
  Further additional points see exercise.
  Recommendation. 10 rounds always: Always 10 rounds

- Integrate the "Golf Mental Breathing" into your routine.
  The "Golf Mental Breathing" will only be applied once on the ball.
  In case of disregard 1 coin will be deducted.

- Variation 1
  In precision practice, the ball must land within a range. Only these balls may be putted.
  CP 3 - CP 5

- Variation 2
  Winning version. Two - Four players or pairs play against each other.
  CP 6 - CP 14

- Variation 3
  Time setting / CP 14

- Variation 4
  Speed / CP-10

- Variation 5
  Shoot-Out. Only the winner enters the next round / CP 13

- Variation 6
  Circle / CP 11, CP 12

CP 1:

- After his shot on the green, the player may putt only twice.
- If successful = 1 coin.

CP 2:

- After his shot on the green, the player may putt only once.
- If successful = 2 Coins.

CP 3:

- After his shot on the green, the ball must remain in a range of 1.5m around the hole.
- The player may putt twice
- If successful = 1 coin.

CP 4:

- After his shot on the green, the ball must remain in a range of 1.5m around the hole.
- The player may putt once.
- If successful = 2 Coins.

CP 5:

- After his shot on the green, the ball must remain in a range of 1.0m around the hole.
- The player may putt once.
- If successful = 3 Coins.

CP 6:

- Three players play against each other against the stopwatch.
- The stopwatch is stopped when the ball has been potted.
- The winner receives 4 coins. The second receives 2 coins. The third 0.
- 5 rounds
- Distance and direction to the hole is set by your golf trainer or a team-mate.

CP 7:

- Like CP 6 + per pass, the distance to the hole varies.

CP 8:

- Like CP 6 + player may putt twice.

CP 9:

- Like CP 6 + player may putt only once.

CP 10:

- Like CP 6 + putt in speed variant, i.e. the player must go to the ball immediately and putt.

CP 11:

- They form player pairs and various CP stations around the training field. The number of stations results from the number of players or the PRO determines the number.
  One player chips, the other putsts. He has only one putt chance.
- Each player has five rounds: 5x chips, 5x putts.
- Each putt has one point.
- Players give their score according to the number of points they have reached.
- Then it goes to the next station.
- Until all stations have been played.
- The winning pair gets 20 extra coins per player,
- The second 15 coins/player, the third 10 coins/player.

CP 12

- Just like CP 11. Only that each player chips and putsts for himself.

CP 13:

- Like CP 2. Various player pairs are formed. Two players play against each other. The winner enters the next round.

- Best of 7 (or Best of 5), i.e. the first player to win four rounds goes into the next round.
- The loser must complete a mental putt exercise, which is not counted.
- The winner gets 20 coins.

CP 14

- Each player has 20 minutes to make as many successful CP´s as possible.

Training Results: **Chip & Putt**

DATE	EXERCISE	RESULTs/ COINS	DATE	EXERCISE	RESULTs/ COINS

Training Results: **Chip & Putt**

DATE	EXERCISE	RESULTs/ COINS	DATE	EXERCISE	RESULTs/ COINS

Training Results: **Chip & Putt**

DATE	EXERCISE	RESULTs/ COINS	DATE	EXERCISE	RESULTs/ COINS

Training Results: **Chip & Putt**

DATE	EXERCISE	RESULTs/ COINS	DATE	EXERCISE	RESULTs/ COINS

Training Results: **Chip & Putt**

DATE	EXERCISE	RESULTs/ COINS	DATE	EXERCISE	RESULTs/ COINS

Training Results: **Chip & Putt**

DATE	EXERCISE	RESULTs/ COINS	DATE	EXERCISE	RESULTs/ COINS

Forecast-Training (FT) & Challenge

As golf trainer, you specify the result to be achieved, which the player must achieve. If the player does not reach the target, the previous PRO gets 1 Euro or ten minus coins are awarded.

The aim of this exercise is to promote concentration, ambition, pressure and stress regulation.

The target is set by the golf trainer.
Forecast means that the player himself sets the goal.
Challenge means that the player can win or lose something.

A. Mental Putts and Chip & Putt
Here there is only one day winner incl. 1 Euro prize from the other players, if the day winner has also reached the target.

B. 9er/18er Flight
Your golf trainer or your fellow player of the flight documents the target and the really achieved goal.

C.
Your golf trainer can also give an exact target for individual holes or all holes. For each completed target the player receives ten coins, for each missed target five coins are deducted.
Coins can also be awarded the other way round.

D.
Your golf trainer as well as other players can veto if the target is set too low. The target must be realistic or a stroke more ambitious.

E.
As a golf trainer, you can set a target from all exercises or have the players themselves define a forecast.

Training Results: **FORECAST**

DATE	EXERCISE + FORECAST	RESULTs/ COINS	DATE	EXERCISE	RESULTs/ COINS

Training Results: **FORECAST**

DATE	EXERCISE + FORECAST	RESULTs/ COINS	DATE	EXERCISE	RESULTs/ COINS

Training Results: **FORECAST**

DATE	EXERCISE + FORECAST	RESULTs/ COINS	DATE	EXERCISE	RESULTs/ COINS

Training Results: **FORECAST**

DATE	EXERCISE + FORECAST	RESULTs/ COINS	DATE	EXERCISE	RESULTs/ COINS

Training Results: **FORECAST**

DATE	EXERCISE + FORECAST	RESULTs/ COINS	DATE	EXERCISE	RESULTs/ COINS

Training Results: **FORECAST**

DATE	EXERCISE + FORECAST	RESULTs/ COINS	DATE	EXERCISE	RESULTs/ COINS

Shoot-Out (SO)

Specifications

- A Shoot-Out can be used as a training module or to play out seats for a league game.

- You can use a Shoot-Out with variant 3 at the end of a training camp or as a one-day training camp.

- 9-hole/18-hole (gross/net as hole or counting game or Staple-ford) plus at least five different exercises from the Mental Handi-cap training program.

- Each hole won = 5 coins.
  Counting game: 100 - Result = Coins.

Shoot-Out

9 / 18 Game Points	EXERCISE	ROUNDS	RESULT	MENTALCOINS opt. Extracoins	TOTAL

Shoot-Out

9 / 18 Game Points	EXERCISE	ROUNDS	RESULT	MENTALCOINS opt. Extracoins	TOTAL

Shoot-Out

9 / 18 Game Points	EXERCISE	ROUNDS	RESULT	MENTALCOINS opt. Extracoins	TOTAL

Shoot-Out

9 / 18 Game Points	EXERCISE	ROUNDS	RESULT	MENTALCOINS opt. Extracoins	TOTAL

Shoot-Out

9 / 18 Game Points	EXERCISE	ROUNDS	RESULT	MENTALCOINS opt. Extracoins	TOTAL

www.golfmentalhandicap.com

Shoot-Out

9 / 18 Game Points	EXERCISE	ROUNDS	RESULT	MENTALCOINS opt. Extracoins	TOTAL

MENTAL COIN SYSTEM

Mental Coin System

EXERCISE	COIN System		EXTRACOINS
Mental Putts	**MP 1 - 10**	Every Putt 1 Coin	All Putts, f.e. 50 = 100% = 10 Coins 47-49 = 94 – 99,9% = 8 Coins 45-46 = 90 – 93,9% = 5 Coins
Pirat Putts	**PP 1 - 10**	Every Putt 1 Coin	All Putts, f.e. 50 = 100% = 10 Coins 47-49 = 94 – 99,9% = 8 Coins 45-46 = 90 – 93,9% = 5 Coins
Winning Putts	**WP 1 - 10**	Every Putt 1 Coin	The Winner = 10 Coins extra
Blind Putts	**BP 1 - 6**	Every Putt 1 Coin	
	BP 7	Every Putt 10 Coins	
	BP 8	Every Putt 20 Coins	
Chip & Putts	**CP 1**	Every Putt 1 Coin	
	CP 2	Every Putt 2 Coins	
	CP 3	Every Putt 1 Coin	
	CP 4	Every Putt 2 Coins	
	CP 5	Every Putt 3 Coins	
	CP 6 - 10	Winner 5 Coins, Second 3, Third 1 per Round	
	CP 11	Every Putt 1 Coin	Winner 20, Second 15, Third 10
	CP 12	Every Putt 1 Coin	Winner 20, Second 15, Third 10
	CP 13	Every Putt 1 Coin	Winner 20
	CP 14	Every Putt 1 Coin	
Forecast	**FT 1**	FP fulfilled 10 Coins / not fulfilled: minus 5 Coins	
	FT 2	FP fulfilled 5 Coins / not fulfilled -10 Coins	
	FT 3	Every FP partly fulfilled 10 Coins / not fulfilled: minus 5 Coins	
	FT 4	Every FP partly fulfilled 5 Coins / not fulfilled: minus 10 Coins	
Shoot-Out	**SO 1**	Every winning whole = 5 Coins.	
	SO 2	Couting game: 100 points minus result = Coins.	

MENTAL COIN TRAININGS PLANNER

(e.g. in a TRAININGSCAMP)

Mental Coin **Training Planner**

EXCERCISE AND FORECAST	MC-Max	MC RESULTS / DAYS						
		1	2	3	4	5	6	7
TOTAL RESULT								

RANKING: _____   TOTAL POINTS: _____   AVERAGE/DAY: _____

Mental Coin **Training Planner**

EXCERCISE AND FORECAST	MC-Max	MC RESULTS / DAYS						
		1	2	3	4	5	6	7
TOTAL RESULT								

RANKING: _____   TOTAL POINTS: _____   AVERAGE/DAY: _____

Mental Coin **Training Planner**

EXCERCISE AND FORECAST	MC-Max	MC RESULTS / DAYS						
		1	2	3	4	5	6	7
TOTAL RESULT								

RANKING: _____   TOTAL POINTS: _____   AVERAGE/DAY: _____

Mental Coin **Training Planner**

EXCERCISE AND FORECAST	MC-Max	MC RESULTS / DAYS						
		1	2	3	4	5	6	7
TOTAL RESULT								

RANKING: _____   TOTAL POINTS: _____   AVERAGE/DAY: _____

Mental Coin **Training Planner**

EXCERCISE AND FORECAST	MC-Max	MC RESULTS / DAYS						
		1	2	3	4	5	6	7
TOTAL RESULT								

RANKING: _____ TOTAL POINTS: _____ AVERAGE/DAY: _____

Mental Coin **Training Planner**

EXCERCISE AND FORECAST	MC-Max	MC RESULTS / DAYS						
		1	2	3	4	5	6	7
TOTAL RESULT								

RANKING: _____ TOTAL POINTS: _____ AVERAGE/DAY: _____

Mental Coin **Training Planner**

EXCERCISE AND FORECAST	MC-Max	MC RESULTS / DAYS						
		1	2	3	4	5	6	7
TOTAL RESULT								

RANKING: _____ TOTAL POINTS: _____ AVERAGE/DAY: _____

Mental Coin **Training Planner**

EXCERCISE AND FORECAST	MC-Max	MC RESULTS / DAYS						
		1	2	3	4	5	6	7
TOTAL RESULT								

RANKING: _____   TOTAL POINTS: _____   AVERAGE/DAY: _____

Mental Coin **Training Planner**

EXCERCISE AND FORECAST	MC-Max	MC RESULTS / DAYS						
		1	2	3	4	5	6	7
TOTAL RESULT								

RANKING: _____ TOTAL POINTS: _____ AVERAGE/DAY: _____

MEMO

MEMO